# STONE | RAIN

# Stone | Rain

POEMS BY

W. H. New

OOLICHAN BOOKS
LANTZVILLE, BRITISH COLUMBIA, CANADA
2001

**Canadian Cataloguing in Publication Data**

New, W.H. (William Herbert), 1938-
   Stone rain

   Poems
   ISBN 0-88982-196-8

   I. Title
PS8577.E776S76 2001   C811'.54     C2001-910503-7

We gratefully acknowledge the support of the Canada Council for the
Arts for our publishing program.

THE CANADA COUNCIL | LE CONSEIL DES ARTS
FOR THE ARTS | DU CANADA
SINCE 1957 | DEPUIS 1957

Grateful acknowledgement is also made to the BC Ministry of Tourism,
Small Business and Culture for their financial support.

We acknowledge the financial support of the Government of Canada
through the Book Publishing Industry Development Program for
our publishing activities.

Canadä

Published by
Oolichan Books
P.O. Box 10, Lantzville
British Columbia, Canada
V0R 2H0

Printed in Canada

*As always*
*for Peggy*

## Acknowledgments

With thanks to Laurie, Alan, and Jack, who read early drafts of some of these poems; and to students and colleagues in China for their generous hospitality; and to Ron, Jay, Hiro, and Linda at Oolichan Books for their enthusiasm and support.

# Contents

# I

## Storyboards

*after seeing the Northwest Coast Mask Exhibit,*
*'Down from the Shimmering Sky,'*
*Vancouver Art Gallery, 1998*

1.

Ulysses anchors offshore
wearing Cook's clothing, Quadra's,
cutting Nootka's seas in four
hemispheres: SEVENTEEN-
SEVENTY-EIGHT—ghosts—
                         NINETY-
THREE: suitors paddle the land
across the mountains, racing winter,
claiming history as theirs,
                         not
listening to the moss,
                         the voices
keening rain *Who's there*

tide's echo: *Who's there*

1.

*Making the masks inscribes alter-*
*natives, carves narratives*
*of being there:*
                    *tree trans-*
*forming into teeth and painted*
*eye, turning wood to shadow*
*stories, spirit, played in breath.*

*What marks the watchers in the art gallery*
*emanates from shadow: takes them out of*
*elsewhere into—*
                    *Listen:*
                              *Ellen*
*Neel's unsighted cedar watching*
*back, talking through the grain . . .*

2.

Prisoners of time:
                    red cedars
hold them at bay, islanded
aboard unfamiliarity—

blinded by expectation, they seek
countryside,
                    stone fences
& portable palms,
                              prospects,
hibiscus & naked invitation.

In this fist of westerlies
landing's out of reach,
                              the strait
home a Brobdingnagian desire.

Distant, the trees begin to drum.

2.

On a television screen
the Edward Curtis film flickers
by, its paddlers, dancers, posed
for authenticity.
                    Set
apart, the masks that Cook collected
stand in a glass case, room
centre, marked 'Nuu-CHAH-NULTH, 18TH
CENTURY, ARTIST UNKNOWN.'
                              Staged
wilderness.
            Outside the glass
anonymity asserts
the universe.
            The forest moves.

3.

Clambering ashore,
                    they step in Selkirk's
image,
          stretching for someone to talk to,
without the words to call this being
into beauty:
              fear
                    flares them, hauls them
into stutter,
              past stone
pebble shell into un-
tongued insubstantiality—

*skookum* eludes them:
                    tidewash resists
their print;
              above them a raven they do not
see ignores their cause, their i-
solating storms, their claim on fable.

*3.*

*Any man saved from drowning*
*(says the guide)'s in further danger:*
*Bak'w̲a̲s lurks in the woods.  Gagiit.*
*He preys on those who flee the ocean,*
*leave the village, drift deep into*
*forest, on their own.*
                                    *Grimacing,*
*four masks stand in a row,*
*warning with skeleton's teeth, the green*
*skin of the mad, of those who lose*
*their place,*

                    *follow the land otter*
*inland,*
            *off the edge of the world.*

4.

Give them two months, three,

                         some
taste the salmonberries,
                    see
the snow rise early on the mountains,
                                    imagine
lotuses must grow on this narrow
band of coast,
                and thirst to stay.


Coho course the rainy rivers,

mussels clasp the rocks:

                         time's
absurd
        & ease
                the thief of history
in this unending spring;

                         the crew
draw water,
                engineer

a soft accord of sea and sky . . .

4.

Hear them, the people,
                    Tlingit, Nishga'a,
Haida, Haisla, Tsimshian, Heiltsuk—
north
          to south—Kwakwaka'wakw,
Nuxalk, Nuuchah'nulth, Salish,
                              each
clan drumming history into myth—
Makah—
          the masks dancing ancestors:
eagle, orca, raven, wolf,
back into time:
                    see the black
wolf, its red side-slash
circumscribing teeth,
                    the better
to celebrate the life of lines.

5.

. . . when out of nowhere a grizzly's lunging
towards them, hump on its back, too
close if they can already see
one eye's been blinded—branch
cougar maybe another bear—

only climbing matters, reach
beyond reach, fir fir
hemlock,
            one slash the claws
strafe the bark sway the trunk
knees lifting higher voice
croaking knuckles hanging on . . .

5.

*Dsónoqua:*
        *she keeps coming back,*
*pendulous, hairy, hollowcheeked,*
*her lips drawn apart, ready*
*to swallow the children she gathers*
*after the flood.*
                *The masks do not*
*show the basket on her back,*
*the bearskin she wears, but the watcher knows them*
*near, hears the giant's footfall*
*paces away from ending—*
                        *Trick*

*of the light—*
                *no:*
                        *for who would dare*
*turn without the warrior's bow.*

19

6.

Circuitously, they come round
to *what upsets them, really,*
       & after
desultory talk—about *the fire*
*of '72, the coming of the great*
*wave before that,* & lava
stories,
   stone seas that over-
turned the world—
      slowly they name
*the others,* always the
       *others,*
        *behaving*
*like pigs,*
    ruining what used
to be as perfect as the moment just
before an old flame returns.

6.

On the wall the transformation
masks hang, hinged slats
and cedar twine as taut as hate.

But the script calls for dancing.
                                    Not
just the elders in the Green Room,
Raven revealing sun, walking
the boards to Heaven:
                        the watchers too,

the theatre of drum, the heart
beat of apprehension ani-
mating spirals,
                    earth turning
Eagle under the shimmering sky.

7.

Croesus-tales,
            rumours of river-
gold,
        ads of land, space,
single spars and
                freedom,
                        hints
of glory,
        promises
                of work,
conversion tables, claims and
                        clapped
hands:
        (words attract still more)


Flotsam.
        Jetsam.
                False prophets.
Ghosts.


        Coal draws them into the
dark, down shafts of under-
ground, sticks, stones, and cold
silica, with no exit but the sun.

7.

*In the undersea room*
*stark masks white as gypsum*
*stroke a copper canoe across*
*carved underwater waves:*

*pale seawolves stir the riptide,*
*blue sharks flex their stone*
*fins, reef, orcas the deep*
*counterpart of air that squalls*
*duality onto the land:*
                              *rain*
*drenches this room, the mind breathes it,*

*along with the sun the blue moon.*

8.

And always another choice to make:

skipper dragging a hemlock boom
past Ripple Rock or Race,

or a pile of kids in a rowboat off
Fisherman's Cove or Dundarave:

or something else:
                    steering clear,
catching the wave, avoiding the grey-
green eddy of preoccupation:

sounding:
            speaking the whitecapped
moment without losing sight
of after:
            *don't go there,*
*world's edge,* they said:
                    *or else*

*8.*

*One of a pair, the stone mask,*
*sightless, sounds undertows—*

*the other, <u>the one with pierced eyes</u>*
*(the caption says) <u>lies abroad:</u>*
*<u>if ever brought together they fit</u>*
*<u>like clasped hands</u>—*

             *the blind stone*
*broods <u>union</u>, dreams <u>meeting</u>,*
*catches memory at the edge of retold*
*tale, the lip of drowning.*
                  *Aboard*
*the strait between otherwise and after,*
*no-one knows the amplitude of waving.*

9.


Fogbanks persist past morning
on the outer shoals;                    ·
                              no-one moves
without compass, gunshot's echo,
strobe's intermittent invi-
tation—
              to storm or safe
harbour, the sirens aboard ship
do not make clear: simply
call *Attention Attention*
                              as though
the shore were underway, ice
vying with argillite, the sea
calm,
              blueprint lit by desire.

9.

'Not the human face divine,'
Cook said, sailing away
with the masks he thought 'shocking,'
                                    leaving
JENNA CASS in his wake: shapes
imagined by the chance to sell—

     DJILAKONS misheard, logged by imi-
     tation into archive:
                         labret-
     extended lips nailed silent,
     no longer noble but 'distorted,'
     bear's teeth 'coarse,' dis-

     carded for the adjective of iron.

10.

Collected, the pelts go too,
into the hold, hauled off
to cattle country, some sunny
distance from the usefulness
of fur.

      Some actors will not dance,
as though they miss the script,
                         cannot
hear the music,
              cannot find
on board the other they're not afraid
to love.

      Yet, even the day of rest,
they round up ache and artefact,

counting beads like an empty trapline.

*10.*

*All falls under the sky*
*and only the strongest arms can fire*
*arrows to the stars.*

*Sun's hands*
*radiate greeting, open*
*mouth breathes language to the land,*
*eyes wide as water shine*
*with abalone brows.*

*The mask-watchers*
*watch themselves growing young:*

*Old man, old woman,*
*climb the arrows,*
*Moon's eyes*
*narrow, dream November snow.*

11.

So many of them pitch then
overboard in thunder—
                    sails
shred, masts crack, the wheel
spins out of reach,
                    lurching
curses, fibre, time against
sisal, muscle, greed.
                    Anian's
crew:    tinker thief sailor:


who's left but the beggarman,
grasping at broken dinghy slats,
glass buoys, cedar mercy,

calling poems to the drifting shore.

11.

*They eat each other from within:*

*that's why the masks dance* <u>Hamatsa</u>—
*against monstrosity*—
                              *dance*
*Crooked-Beak, in raffia and red*
*cedar, to hold back the cannibal-*
*at-the-North-End-of-the-World,*
                                        *dance*
*Thunderbird, who ruffles the inner*
*edges of the sky's extreme,*

*dance Raven, Eagle,*
                          *claim*
*again the earth that shapes them*
*human:*
             *ocean   fire   air.*

12.

Who makes it home after the raft's
slap atop uneven seas,
finds a city already built
upon the green island,
                          the people
lodged in birth and death,
                                forgetting
the traveller, or editing aside
the traveller's return.


                          Memory resists
the real, curtains it as column,
cycle, cage.


                Words know
otherwise,
                float their own Pacific
currents,
                lonely as black stone.

12.

Who makes it home: the carvers—Hunt,
Reid, Seaweed, Neel, Davidson,
Tait, Martin, Edenshaw—
those here and those who are still
here, who live, dancing, in the grain.

Shadow-makers, even during
the night rain, the needle-wind,
they recognize the storyboards,
ask light to play across
the face of forest, write home
in masks: islands, inlets, green.

II

City Limits

❧

## Weed

*Four children stand*
*on the sidewalk's edge*
broom valerian woodruff sedge

*Two by two*
*they stroll apart*
native pipe and bleeding heart

*Three step out*
*and one steps back*
bitterroot in the pavement crack

*Four and none*
*remain to die*
chicory and bearded rye

❧

Fissures

Talk to the old people, they all
remember '48 *the year*
*of the Fraser flood,* or '46
*the year of the last earthquake,* adding
*the last big one anyways*—and tell
Typhoon Frieda stories,
trees falling out of the sky,
Blackout, the Big Strike (whichever),
Bloody Sunday—tell of *the year*
(they can't quite remember) *they*
*took down Blackburns' Market and put up*
*them damn condominiums*
instead. Talk to the old people:
things were bigger then—not
larger, just bigger, more
real than *all the glass-and-concrete*
*they've gone and filled the spaces with*—
maybe it's possibility
they've cached away, maybe some
secret dream of wilderness:
they remember the spaces, the old people,
look back past
emptiness to cameraderie:
houses, horses, nights full of stars,
a time when they didn't tumble,
didn't drown, didn't fall
through the gap the earth opened, back
in the clear, before the tremors began.

# City Limits

GREY
*'I name this point
in compliment to my friend Captain George Grey of the Navy'*
(the other George, Vancouver, ignoring Don
Juan de Langara and the Musqueam nose, *Ulksen*, already there)

FRASER
*Cowitchans' River, Tacoutche Tesse,* the *New Caledonia*
becoming *Fraser's* when Thompson made it so
(Fraser having earlier named the Thompson *Thompson,*
both of them Company men)

BURNABY
Robert, 4th son of the Reverend Thomas, a Leicester man
(unlike the Loyalist Simon, the King's Lynn George, or ruddy David
whose 'speech betrayed the Welshman'), arriving in 1858 with an intro from Bulwer-
Lytton, to search for coal, on a dark and no doubt stormy night

BURRARD
*Boca de Floridablanca* (the politics of knowing who knows who), supplanted
by another friend of George's, this one Sir Harry, RN,
who changed his name to marry an heiress who ladied-in-wait on the queen,
*Charlotte,* her of the Islands-in-hiding, who made him Admiral

GEORGIA
Strait goods define the city's limits:
shelled cliffs, salmoned reaches, firred forest, musselled shore—
glory channelled into transit patterns, traffic,
surveyors' names restaked in dotted lines

Terminal City

Building the railroad through the Fraser Canyon
had to start somewhere or else end
        *She knew she was dying*
        *and then him too*
never Craigellachie though that's where
Sir William pounded down the iron spike
        *but refused the thin gruel*
        *of hopelessness*
and not the port at Moodyville despite
the glacial sea.  It had to be west of there
        *kept looking for a different cure*
        *a better place*
that's where the coal seam was and the bits of land
the Three Greenhorns turned into property
        *loving life enough*
        *to resist leaving*
That's when Shaughnessy could be parcelled
into protective custody.  Not a bad day's work
        *not knowing what strength*
        *they'd need*
if you could get it.  The Depression came later
food strikes     the Riot Act     riding the rods
        *grit scattering ash*
        *on blank sand*

# Timing

Something changed when they moved Birks' Corner,
took away the clock: they just
shifted it a few blocks north,
but that removed the meeting place

and no-one stops there any more—
Funny, how you take things for granted:
Woodward's, Scott's, the Honey Dew,
they all disappear—and even Birks

got sold: you couldn't afford to shop there,
but even in rain the windows glistened—
and the clock, one of those iron Edwardian
contraptions, lighted face on a pedestal,

satisfied some need for ornament
in a world at war, made meeting
still possible when it didn't seem
as though it could be—and then, after, you forgot—

forgot you needed to meet—and suddenly
all that's left is the space you thought
you wanted, and the wind tunnel, and a distant glimpse
of lindentree and turning the time of day.

Cabbage Roses

*There's not enough time,* they said
*never enough*: wanting to finish—
something—giving their lives over to
*in a minute, in a minute*—

mad dashes turning into
decades and before they know it    ends
and a time to forget.  The old preacher
knew a thing or two—knew

the season to reap   the season to sow—
collapsing days of death and being
born—run into each other
out of reach and into letting go.

He just never mentioned
the time to forget: it has its own
season—one of wicker baskets and withered
rosemary—cauliflower in a polished bowl.

## Counting Day

Asked how she feels to be 103
the old nun answers *quelquefois deux cent trois,*
slurring her words, so it's hard to hear
if she's giving youth to God
or claiming middle age.

Either way, she laughs with God in mind
at all the forms in front of her
(and memories of the other callers
who at 20, 40, 80,
stiff, unbending, bent,
tried to woo her with roses and epaulets,
Youth-for-Christ medallions
and tales of meeting Goddard and the Northwest Mounted).

She minds them all, watching still 20-20
at the table laid before her, sure
as the lovers at Khajuraho and Herculaneum
of leaping one day, whole, from here to heaven.

The enumerator's one of many in the latter days—
colour commentators, would-be writers
of her long life (resistance is embrace)—
but all *he* needs to ascertain
is if she's old enough to vote, and what she owns.
*De mes yeux, rien,* she says. *Ouais; Dieu me réclame.*
How does it feel, he asks, uncertain then
if what he's heard is measurement or grace,
and if his questionnaire is worth completing.

Her eyes refuse objection; lips close,
laugh lines intact; skin,
what you see of it, settles,
folding slowly, like origami birds.

## Placing the Stress

*Did she have an accent?* the children ask
about Grandmother-they-never-knew,
who'd died of pneumonia, typhus, in childbirth,
before penicillin certainly, in the flu epidemic
of '17, during the War—and their father,
the grandmother's son, himself already old,
pauses: listens against the strains of Brandenburg
drifting from the next room, Vivaldi's *Seasons,*
too soft to tell exactly, Elgar, the Yellow River
Symphony, the tape rolling its own ocean
until he says *Yes,* but the voice is puzzled,
knows the answer without remembering it—
*yes,* he says, maybe meaning *no,*
*I know what you want but cannot place the moment*
*the familiar began to sound strange.*

Later the children, parents themselves, find
they can recognize without question separate
infant voices in the night, differentiate
hunger from rumbling discontent, tell hurt
from playground peal, isolate the timbre
in the past-midnight telephone call that mumbles
*Hi,* and tacks on *It's me,* as though
a second wave of syllables might clarify
without declaring need—all this time
fretting about landfall displacing shore. Then
*What did grandfather sound like?* one of them asks,
finding the old tape when they're clearing out
the house. *Did you keep what he said?* turning on
the out-of-date machine to listen: *Yes*
it whispers foreign, meaning maybe *no.*

## Pieces of Eight

Saturday night at 6:30—it's a Rockwell cover
at the White Spot on Broadway, the whole city's
eating, two cops in the first booth
drinking tea, getting a leg up
on overdue reports, so's not to stay late;
the math teacher and two of her friends, dividing
the bill by 3, minus GST, adding
the tip outside the brackets;
                        the waitress
knows them all, the Mrs. Bailey's dinner,
the pirate pak, the small salad with extra
ranch, the usual with Special Sauce—
                              longshoreman,
coach, exotic dancer ('here last night,'
the postman says, 'in mufti'):
                      the 4-year-old
Punjabi kid dancing by the door, singing
*Silent Night* and *Rudolph the Red-Nosed Reindeer*—

*Legendary*'s the word they use.


                      How
the world began, perhaps, or why the winter's
cold.
        The scent of fried onion drowns
the woollen damp of overcoats.  Blind
Pew could follow his nose here, rap
his cracked cane against the window without
going in, dispense his black message
on silver's sidewalks—crooning *rum*
and rasping out his hand for spare change.

## Miles from Anywhere

Roy Arden's photograph
buries in bushes
a sign that says SLOW—
Hard to know
if the bushes are listening

Other signs flash subliminal truths
Lowry's SHELL with the s blinking—
NO EXIT parked in the supermarket lot
next to the telephone booth—
poor Superman

Millennial, this preoccupation
with knowing—pointing fingers,
burning shrubs, the hand-
lettering outside the tropical greengrocers
PASSIONS    4 FOR A DOLLAR

## Agnostic

Grizzled, impatient, perpetually unconvinced,
he's taken on weight and desperation
together, as though substance lied, inconstant
as particles, the syntax of moment confused
by the counterploy of motion. Treading forward,
coffee cup in hand, covered against
unlikelihood, he twists to look back—
the matter he seeks eluding him. Just
the strength to keep moving, perhaps—or go
back—refusing *either*, rejecting *all*,
and never sure: traces of play—figures
from a past he cannot trust, random
as blood oranges—wall him in adverbs
and sudden salt. Hermit, halted in mid-
air, he's the ninth man, crossed
by fools' errands and lightless formulas,
limping towards origins, or maybe end.

## Sherwood Urban

The guy with the cell phone
leans back beneath an old
tin Robin Hood Flour sign
against a faux-log-cabin wall
in Calhoun's

            Amused
at something he listens to
or is it something clever
he's just heard himself say
he lolls—

               inflates—

               disengages—

toys with a croissant crust
a last sip of cappuccino
                 then
saunters bowlegged  under
the exit sign in the garrison wall
looking both ways
                out on the sidewalk
for Nottingham

Drawstring

The young woman with orange hair
wrestles with the lawn mower
push struggling with shove

finally says *Hi*
asks for help     reluctantly
not anxious to seem Not Strong     Not
Competent     Not Anything maybe     Not
Anxious to seem Anxious certainly  or even Not

It's a girl & guy thing     learning how to be cool
in the nineties
Fahrenheit of course

*Hi*

Even the unmechanical ought to know the
first ropes     know the gradient has to be level
to start with     know how far
ignition lies from absolutely zero
how quickly pressure repeated floods the engine
breaks the cord

The trick is to make it look easy
without making it look simple
the sophistication of a pull-toy
in Mazatlan
green as alfalfa in a field of clay

*I can take it from here*  she says

## Strange Comfort

Asked about landslides
the architect assures us
our fears our groundless

The doctor says
the only moles to worry about
are ones like this

But there are compensations:
signs of Free Trade everywhere
spell out

professional jealousies:
the engineer wears aviator shades
the pilot wears a truss

# Blue Streak

Hard words from the management
at Head Office, when they send out (by e-mail)
the rules for their essay contest in MEN'S
HEALTH: (1) *Do not belittle;*
(2) *Write about yourself, but connect*
*with the larger male picture.*

                    You wonder
which picture they have in mind—
the one at the English soccer match
perhaps, the bobby holding his blue
helmet in front of a Sixties streaker,
*Oh Calcutta, Hair,* the *Full*
*Monty:* Prospero thumbing through
Gray's Anatomy.

                    You wonder, if
to enter, you have to sign with an X,
send your entry in an unmarked envelope,
and who, anyway, endowed the competition.

You know

the yuppies are middleaged when it's très chic
to hang out after jazzercise at any
weekend hour you care to name with latte,
two friends, the dog and his water dish,
and watch the locals stroll by in shades;

when the Sunday morning jogging club knows
all the words to anything by Nana Mouskouri
and the Everly Brothers, and when a good half of them,
later, gather justified at Sweet
Obsessions for crême brulée and a simple tisane;

when the pastry shop opens in the same block
as the organic grocery; when grey's okay for sideburns
but not bright enough to wear, arugula's
a social weapon, and after sex
talk turns to carpal tunnel syndrome.

They savour their brioche moments, knowing these last
as long as espresso jolts and pet rock
passion, but no longer, and no longer caring:
none of them has room to bossa nova
any more, however the rhythms play.

Anyway, the Y Generation's
already moving into unfinished suites
in some place different, what else is new,
finding space for the cds, and clearing away
the hula hoops from the basement corner.

Pet Theory

Imagine the tyrants at home
        wrapped in the blankets of dailiness—
        Genghis walking the Pekingese, Ivan the Afghan
        on a long lead—

The travellers, preoccupied with magnitude
        (rubies the size of oranges, exploding
        paper, volumes bound with silver clasps)
        never mention the dogs—

Maybe Marco didn't like them, maybe
        Vasco was allergic, and Sam and Chris and Frank
        all left town to get away from the collies
        and corgis and crossbred strays—

Oh yes, cats—cats everywhere—
        panthers, jaguars, lionkings, sleek ocelots
        and all those independent obelisks, tiger-eyed
        and prone, you'd expect cats—

But supposing they'd noticed the dogs—
        you could rewrite history through spaniel eyes,
        the telegraphic tail, the slobbering grin:
        *wanna play ball, Genghis?  Hey Ivan, fetch?*

It wouldn't work, though, tossing out hyperbole,
        filling in with bland: it's always the ordinary
        you can't come to terms with, the terrible ambiguity
        of the power to say no.

## Sixteen Sidewalks

### 1

The plank is slippery     Mosses twist
on paving stones     Nettle snatches
fabric back from a sinuate path

### 2

A place to be      or a track to get
somewhere else     the word on the street
chokecherry      metaphor

### 3

Tossed tokens occupy
one square at a time      Dandelions
take root in the space between

### 4

Street cycles     rounding the corners
push chair to motorized
scooter     with or without trainers

5

Snow:    flakes    packs    pleats
plats    sheets    obliterates
invites     hikers into the street


6

Rutting    sodded earth breaking
open    Hooker's Evening Primrose
scenting the corner    worn frail


7

The eyes sidle from recognition
drop into distance    attach attitude
to touch    contact    skirting the issue


8

Outsiders (inevitably)
living here    The ads for the strippers
ask passersby to Come On In

9

Lined by lines    the road narrows
by marquees    NO SOLICITING
RING FOR ANSWER    NO SHOES . . .


10

Eating there    green olives
and checkerboard    lace and Sally
Lunn    the other Sally's kitchen


11

Perimeter    nearness sounding the difference
about and around    the voiceless border
between civilized and free


12
Panhandlers drum Mozart where
vetch clambers    scout the bins
next to the tubs of California poppies

13

The pawnshop operator     pulls
down the steel grate     the teller
asks for collateral     cheek by jowl


14

Four walk abreast in the other
direction     forcing one into
wild timothy     onto the verge


15

Traffic frames the action     dis-
regarding motion     clover and blind
cane tapping at the concrete curb


16

Saree silk spills over
the window ledge     Coriander
like colour     refuses a closed room

≈

### Right of Way

The new garden guide
shows four ways in full colour
how to plant, through your woods,
a walk for all seasons:

how to pollard also,
draw bees,
arrange rocks for nature's sake
in casual measure—

Repose: there's the word—the caption says
the king admired camas in the forest so much
he got his gardener to give them more exposure,
plant 3000 of them in his grove:

None along the railway, though,
track disappearing in scrub and dust—
nor does the book explain
why it's there,

in tangles,
          wild
blackberries grow,
sweet and thorn.

≈

Absence

Before the world began
stars boiled in a sky
that did not know it was sky
nor they stars

Pterodactyls screamed
on splayed fingers, unable
to count their own measure

No rain rained
No sun brushed
with ecstasy their wings

Before the world began
you were not here

>     *Imagine:*
>     *imagine nothing:*
>     *void waiting to fill*
>
>     *a stir of dancing absolutes*
>     *unhoused      without dimension*
>
>     *number     word     meaning*
>     *standing still in fraction*
>
>     *imagine the metrics of absence*
>     *unfused*

imagine linearity lost
the sea spare
the land blank     air
unbreathable as pain

                              If

you are not there

the world before the world
began is wordless      stars
cannot fly nor random
particles dream equation

there     outside the mind
beyond the fingertips
stones     do not learn
to swim

## Pacific Rim

They can scarcely imagine the outer coast,
those who live inland: the Strait
holds them in tow, learned ridges
still their air until all doubt,
demand, dissolve in breathlessness.

On the outer coast, a pod of orcas
surfaces and dives, a seiner
cables against uncertain weather,
breakers trip electrically
from lap to lash against the barnacles

and abalone shell. Glass fishing
floats at high tidemark tell
of China off horizon's edge, centuries'
silicon polished in fire,
stranded here in kelp and severed

spruce—they punctuate the grey
intensity of sea, the green
bones of the sandstone sealyard:
here dolphins crest the ocean's
skin, skim immerse and skim,

embracing the storm. Inland, acceptance
turns arrangement into nature.
On the outer coast, order's
unreal, the strip of tidewash
the near ledge only of knowing

where landfall lies. Those who live here
understand that clamshell cracks,
tsunami swallows, rockfall kills
in thunder: choosing rim, refusing circle's
centre, wade the intertide.

Stone bench, crevice, tree

1.
A bicycle by a stone bench:
   the one woman resting there
   turns pages in a physics text

2.
Under the arch of the moongate:
   a matriarch in brocade jacket
   laughs at a girl in tennis shorts

3.
Sculpture park      weathered limestone:
   three children in blue tracksuits
   play to its voices      classic rock

4.
Locust flowers on a clay path:
   the sweeper piles dead branches
   in the courtyard like four paper fans

5.
Vine      mapping the creviced border:
   five students from the university
   change the world      Taoist koans

6.
Six roses in a Chinese garden:
    one bleeds against the back
    of a courting couple in black silk


7.
Grey smoke from the great wall:
    seven boys from the middle school
    boast of perfection    a game of pearl


8.
Air caressing the pond water:
    eight men practise *qi gong*
    their hands walking a path to hilltop

## Feed Me

The lone American who wanders
hungry in the garden talks
money, Navy, the CIA
and the new wife he's just saved
for democracy and capitalism, the two houses
he already owns in Oregon,
the cost of the down payment, words
like *hundreds, thousands* dropping with every
breath.
      *Saving face,* he says,
*delays progress by decades,*

and stays to talk about the white
rabbit he's just bought for ten yuan,
keeping it from the stew pot:
he brings it in a backpack to the sculpture park
to feed.
      His father-in-law has blessed
the marriage, he says, and muses *that's
the first time* he's ever called him
*father-in-law . . .*
        *but I guess he is . . .*

His wife has changed already, he says,
and talks of taking her to Disneyworld.

The rabbit nibbles at a lettuce weed,
eyes darting everywhere,
looking for Alice.

Payne's Grey

A line of light falls sideways
after rain
lies on the water     idle
as saint's aura
hovering

the outstretched arm     the painter uttering
Buddha's enigmatic blessing
*May you live*     moment
moment     *without hope*

Catch the brushwork
touch air     the afterglow
of varnish     each
change of signature
vanishes under lead white frame

the Strait sky louvring the west
the long look of no-one special
drawing bitterns
onto open sea

Stroke: speech register

The old dictionary falls to pieces, pages
not acid-free, cracking, words con-
tracting into suffixes, whole
songlines dropping incontinent to ash.

The rain hurts, eats meaning out of house
and garden. *Zinnia* disappears. So does
*chimney*, liederless as smoke on a bare stage,
*Schubert, hubris, husband, hatrack, bard—*

*Trombones overhead, flying not-north*
*to the ribcage, other's nitric, picket night light*
in the narrow dark, terror's
dislocated latitude the length of loss.

When islands drown, even Atlas fails
to hold the mountains: *understanding, recognition,*
signatures of consequence fade: plastic nametags
left instead, standing cogs, icons—

Czerny exercises for the keyboard's one
note, burnt to monosyllables: no
*am* no *on* no *at* no *in* no *if . . .*

In Blue, in the Graveyard

Laying the old man to rest,
his favourite old fedora on the coffin,
the family stand close,
preoccupied in black with lilac and white heather,

stand aside, remembering
when the future was not yet here,
the day of the last death still to come:
not yet telling the day of the next.

Meanwhile, the under-twos
wander away from exhortation,
step jauntily from stone to stone, imp-
rovise the moment, dance in blue;

they roll down
grassy hollows, clamber out, crow
magnitudes
and do it again.

Later (if there is later) all of them gather
in anecdote and red wine, disclaiming
clay, but knowing no-one now ahead of them
deferring.

At the graveside next their own
a child's particoloured toy, planted
abruptly in the earth,
plays with the current,

squeals impulsively.
Abandoned
catherine wheel.
Erratic wind.

## Figure-Eights

The sandpipers sing in eighth-notes—
fall waving in like fog on a lee shore,
alders yellowing, black poplars
shedding back to bark and umber bud.

Under the camouflage of evening
sandpipers sing in eighth-notes, darting,
solitary knots curling
in flight, circling to the same salt ponds

as though tied to their beginnings.
Alpha. Alpha. Truncated speech:
the sandpipers sing in eighth-notes,
their roles dreamt or memorized in motion.

Belief has seasons: *all, almost,*
*not at all, the edge of never, all,*
thin as the sound of fog or bright
as streaked sandpipers, singing eighth-notes.

Somewhere on air or ice, a single
skater practises infinity,
the blade quavering, concentrating
posture, alive as ocean in the cold,

while sandpipers sing in eighth-notes,
praising crustacean, complaining of lost
alfalfa fields, or just turning radar
to the perfect possibility of return.

# III
# Bicycle Rack

1.

All bicycles are black:
no, not all: a pink one
leans on the shed in the open market
where the woman in grey sells pens,
and two boys on blue racers show off
on a side road, shoulders down
to fly ahead. But no one stands out
like the middleaged man on a black bicycle
moving methodically through traffic with a potted
hibiscus in his wire carrier, its one
red flare bracing the wind.

2.

At 7 a.m. on a Wednesday morning, forty-
four people go by in less
than a minute, cycling to work and school,
their faces as impassive as Yang
figurines moulded in clay: scholar,
fortune-teller, cobbler, baker,
in Nikes and blue uniform.
One young lover pedals
dreamily, his eyes inward. Perched
side-saddle behind him, his girlfriend,
legs crossed, polishes her nails.

### 3.

The courtyard fills first with calm,
the students of *tài dà* moving
balance from hand to hand, while one
graceful woman circles backwards
slowly round the whole square,
her arms gliding like birds. Then
breakfast cooks appear, in white hats
and aprons, gesturing anecdote
and smoking. By 8 the yard is empty,
but it's racked in bicycles, the act of change
unspoken, like the instant a lotus opens.

### 4.

Strains of *Swan Lake* lift
off a loudspeaker, but the bicycle
riders move as though deaf to dying.
Like filaments of tide, they weave through traffic,
the man with a sack of rice on his back,
the window-framer, the woman in orange
carrying glass. But nothing is clear:
the glazier steers with one hand,
the other shouldering a rusted iron
pipe. They dance, the *corps de ballet*,
to a different music, living here.

5.
*'Long divided, the empire must*
*unite; long united must*
*divide.'* It's the young who laugh.
The middleaged affect a neutral gaze,
knowing the recent world too well.
The young on their bicycles think themselves
the Yellow Scarves, the moment's rebels,
certain today the round world
will not wheel. The old project
*zhì huì*, Han wisdom, recalling
*The Three Kingdoms*, how it ends and begins.


6.
Two men lean over a boy
in the barber's chair: he scowls his chin
into the white sheet on his chest.
It's a scene from a sidewalk pantomime:
the bicycle, flinging past, catching
the barber in mid-clip, the two men
stretching to measure the boy, the boy
weighing the pros and cons of howling . . .
‾ Maybe.   No crowd gathers.
Likely the eye invents action
where unaccustomed stillness plays.

7.

At the edge of the standing bicycles
outside the bookstore, beside the bank
and near the underpass, country
people spread copies of pop pics
on the sidewalk: *Titanic* posters, old
magazines, small libraries
of plastic wrap and dust. Some men
squat to read; few buy.
Behind them, doors open, close:
the city, massing motion, speeds
riders into a melee of horns.


8.

Confucius sits at the brick gate
watching the world without depending
on it: must be Confucius, the eyes
speak survival, the hard years
and the inevitability of going on
(like the cardboard man: the one who gathers
boxes, flattens them on the back
of his black bicycle, and rounds his way
*fen* by *fen* from ricebowl into dark):
except he knows and does not see
the tightening string about the world.

9.
At 4 in the afternoon a single
customer eats *jiaozi*
at the outdoor restaurant. Under
the canopy other patrons sit
wrapped in wrinkled concentration,
still, until a swift pounce
at the Chinese chess board stirs
a brief *aaah,* and a slap of cards
at another table answers. An old
woman sits facing the street,
watching inward, ignoring the bicycles.


10.
The scholar tells a story about
a snake, kept for a year in a bottle
of wine, alive—that sank its fangs
in the hand of the man who opened the lid.
The snake was poisonous. The man died.
*A true story,* the scholar says,
*It happened in the South.* Faraway narratives—
the bicycle thief who takes Grandfather's
ashes, the scorpion who steals eggs—
all sting slowly, the tale
curled gently on the teller's tongue.

11.
The *Analects* define *lì*
as propriety as well as ritual, recognizing
order as agreed-upon perception,
time's by-product, appearance.  In the morning
the cyclists who pedal fishnets of produce
into the market know disguise
is all.  Pear-apples, cucumbers, arriving
wrapped, turn by arrangement into
exhibition.  Life is allegory,
every street a shuffle of ancients'
proverbs, a route to ambiguity.


12.
*Balance*: the word is *balance*: under
a pink umbrella, the pedicab driver
lurches his passengers through traffic
over to road right, pacing
his forward moves, backpedalling at corners,
steering close to the curb.  He ignores
the painted lines, knowing like everyone
else how colour fades.  But carries
a talisman—Kuan Yin, floating
on a lotus petal, compassion shading
the world: undusted in decades, she smiles.

### 13.

Outside, the gardeners renew
the earth around the rose trees,
but no birds sing. Inside, the flute
player and the master of *suo nà*
coax birds into the air
already warbling, imaginary treetops
drawing them up to a canopy
of counterpoint. Outside, a cleaner dredges
bicycle tires from a fetid canal.
Somewhere a seminar gathers,
trying to remember the sound of the phoenix.


### 14.

At night the bicycles disappear
into a waterhiss of wheels
turning, lightless, in the dark.
Even past midnight, the streets
move, sleepless, sound meaning
motion but not motion sound.
Voices carry. No-one speaks:
leaf and path alive with riders,
bush and bench alive with lovers.
Toads croak. Shadow bends.
The scent of jasmine hides the moon.

15.

The women who ride bicycles rise
early, leave by 6 for the hour's
trip to where they work: bank,
bar, computer factory. Some
jobs are uniformed: the women
who sell silk and lipstick live
all day in gloss and blue apron;
the tellers count *kuài* in brown.
Behind doors and walls, some
are uniformed, steaming rice,
mending cotton, rising by six.


16.

And others live their passions openly
twined in embrace. Angry. Laughing.
Jasmine in yellow pantsuit. Weeping
over the world ending, with a onetime friend
slumped nearby looking hard
or relieved or ashamed. Or singing
out loud to celebrate being
able to sing out loud. Sometimes
it's deliberate. Sometimes it's just
not knowing what else
to do but step on the pedal and go.

17.

The new bicycles in the market
still have their treaded tires wrapped
in plastic. By the next stall
an enterprising salesman washes
old bikes for a fee, makes them
shine again for the moment before
grime. Everything returns here
smooth: grass, paper, stone,
the unemployed in the underground
labour exchange, the proverbs that pedal
softly, separating want from need.


18.

The carriers on bicycle backs
hold the whole heart of industry:
two sheets of thin plywood,
detritus from a building site,
bricks, punnets, baskets full of
watermelons, soccer balls
tied together, young children,
old mothers, halt and lame.
The *foreign experts* carry with them
just their cases, loaded high
with oracles and paperclips and gum.

19.
The policeman in brown uniform, shoes
polished, cap set at a smart
correct angle, navigates
his bicycle through a parody picture-show,
wanting *just the bit of in
formations please* before the shoot.
At sea in the other's tongūe, ħung up
on *tine* and *propositions*, they gesture
their way past tenterhooks, to a second
reel, trading scrip and cutting
roles to order *indirection*.


20.
Walking with a bicycle is dangerous, the spin
of possibility as narrow as irises,
as raw as isolation. The sky
is flat, the road a bowl of speed
and rainless days. The margins rut
with jostle, and clay cakes underfoot:
exhaust clips one side,
hawkers the other, cough and tossed
waterbowl both caught in mid-air,
kiln-dried, ash. At the edge
of connection the walker's eyes tire.

21.
Abandoned bicycles gather in the outer
court of Confucius Temple. Across
the bridge of the pan pool, marble
carving itself, all is silent.
Taxi horns recede. Dust
grows on the lutes and bells in the Inner
Hall, and even the *bian jeng*,
tinplate phoenixes perched on its crossbar,
hangs still. Despite the blue
ceiling, where dragons dance gilded
riddles, the birds wait longer to burn free.


22.
Down streets, lanes, alleys
every sidewalk market sports
a bicycle repairman. All men,
some arranging brake shoes, locks
and handlebars, most content with pump
and patches, a waterbowl nearby
to test for air. The elegant woman
whose tire bursts outside the Workers'
Museum spurns them all; the garnet
silk's deceptive: she fixes her own,
inflating, calm, on platform soles.

23.
Straddling her bicycle, the young woman
from Hunan offers help,
partly to practise her English, mainly
to be kind, and then flies off, crossing
traffic as easily as culture, into
a flap of non-linear equations:
chaos comes alive here: all
energy's expressed in motion, light
converting heat, the taxicabs
straddling lines to get ahead,
the wings of the butterfly predicting sun.


24.
Then there are those the bicycle
passes, the barrowmen who elude
understanding: the one with two
snakes coiled in waterbottles,
who sits staring at a writhing tray
of silkworms; the one with castoff quotations
bound in red tatters; the one
with white gloves, fishing twisted
dough from vats of steam. Into
the air they go, only imagined,
turning and turning and turning into dream.

## ABOUT THE AUTHOR

W. H. New was born in Vancouver and attended UBC and the University of Leeds. For eighteen years, he was the editor of the distinguished critical quarterly, *Canadian Literature*. He has lectured and taught in Australia, India, Italy, China, France and the USA, and held the Brenda & David MacLean Chair in Canadian Studies at UBC.

OTHER BOOKS BY W.H. NEW

SCIENCE LESSONS (1996)
RAUCOUS (1999)